G.W.

Mastering Your Money

Practical Budgeting Tips for Financial Success

First edition

This book was professionally typeset on Reedsy.
Find out more at reedsy.com

"The slightest adjustments to your daily routines can dramatically alter the outcomes in your life."

– DARREN HARDY

Contents

1

Introduction

Explanation of the importance of budgeting

Budgeting is a fundamental aspect of personal finance management that plays a crucial role in achieving financial stability, security, and success. Here's a detailed explanation of why budgeting is so important:

Financial Awareness: Budgeting allows individuals to gain a clear understanding of their financial situation. By tracking income and expenses, individuals become more aware of their spending habits, financial priorities, and areas for improvement. This awareness is the first step toward making informed financial decisions.

Goal Setting: Budgeting helps individuals set and achieve their financial goals. Whether it's saving for a down payment on a house, paying off debt, or planning for retirement, a budget serves as a roadmap for allocating resources toward specific objectives. Without a budget, it's easy to lose sight of financial goals and struggle to make progress.

Expense Management: Budgeting enables individuals to control their spending and live within their means. By creating spending limits for various expense categories (such as housing, groceries, transportation, entertainment, etc.), individuals can prioritize their spending based on their financial goals and values. This helps prevent overspending, reduce debt, and build savings over time.

Emergency Preparedness: Budgeting helps individuals prepare for unexpected expenses and financial emergencies. By setting aside funds for emergencies in a savings account or emergency fund, individuals can mitigate the impact of unforeseen events such as medical emergencies, car repairs, or job loss. Having a financial safety net provides peace of mind and reduces financial stress during difficult times.

Debt Management: Budgeting is essential for managing debt effectively. By incorporating debt payments into their budget and allocating extra funds toward debt repayment, individuals can accelerate their progress toward becoming debt-free. A budget also helps individuals avoid accumulating additional debt by identifying and addressing spending patterns that contribute to debt accumulation.

Wealth Building: Budgeting is a key tool for building wealth and achieving long-term financial success. By consistently saving and investing a portion of their income, individuals can grow their wealth over time and achieve financial independence. A budget helps individuals prioritize saving and investing, allowing them to build a solid financial foundation for the future.

Financial Freedom: Ultimately, budgeting empowers individuals to take control of their finances and achieve financial freedom. By living within their means, avoiding unnecessary debt, and making strategic financial decisions, individuals can create a lifestyle that aligns with their values and priorities. Financial freedom means having the flexibility and resources to pursue opportunities, pursue passions, and enjoy life on your own terms.

In summary, budgeting is essential for achieving financial stability, security, and success. It provides individuals with the tools and framework they need to manage their finances effectively, achieve their goals, and build a brighter financial future.

Overview of the book's purpose and structure

Purpose:

"Mastering Your Money" is designed to provide readers with practical guidance and actionable strategies to take control of their finances through effective budgeting. The book aims to empower readers to make informed financial decisions, set and achieve their financial goals, and ultimately achieve financial freedom and success.

Structure:

This book is structured to provide readers with a comprehensive guide to budgeting, covering everything from basic principles to advanced techniques for achieving financial success. Each section offers practical advice, tips, and strategies, supported by real-life examples and actionable steps to help readers apply the concepts discussed.

By following the guidance outlined in this book, readers can gain confidence in managing their finances, overcome financial challenges, and ultimately master their money for a brighter financial future.

2

Understanding Budgeting Basics

Definition of a budget

Definition of a budget:

A budget is a financial plan that outlines an individual's or organization's expected income and expenses over a specific period, typically monthly, quarterly, or annually. It serves as a roadmap for allocating financial resources to various categories such as housing, food, transportation, debt repayment, savings, and entertainment, among others.

Key components of a budget include:

Income: This refers to the money received from sources such as salaries, wages, investments, rental income, and any other sources of revenue.

Expenses: These are the costs incurred for goods and services necessary for daily living or business operations. Expenses may include fixed expenses (e.g., rent, mortgage, insurance premiums) and variable expenses (e.g., groceries, utilities, entertainment).

Savings and Investments: This category represents the portion of income allocated for saving towards future goals, building an emergency fund, retirement savings, or investing in assets such as stocks, bonds, or real estate.

Debt Payments: If applicable, a budget includes funds allocated for repaying debts such as credit card balances, student loans, mortgages, or car loans.

Discretionary Spending: This category includes non-essential expenses such as dining out, travel, entertainment, and luxury items. Discretionary spending can vary based on individual preferences and financial priorities.

The primary purpose of a budget is to help individuals or organizations manage their finances effectively, ensure that expenses do not exceed income, and work towards achieving financial goals.

By creating and adhering to a budget, individuals can track their spending, identify areas for cost-cutting or improvement, prioritize financial goals, and ultimately achieve greater financial stability and success.

Additionally, budgets provide a basis for evaluating financial performance, making informed financial decisions, and adapting to changes in income or expenses over time.

Importance of setting financial goals

Setting financial goals is crucial for several reasons:

Clarity and Direction: Financial goals provide clarity and direction in managing personal or organizational finances. They give a clear sense of what one wants to achieve financially, whether it's buying a house, saving for retirement, paying off debt, or starting a business. Without clear goals, it's easy to drift aimlessly and lose focus on long-term financial priorities.

Motivation and Focus: Setting specific, measurable, achievable, relevant, and time-bound (SMART) financial goals helps to motivate individuals or teams to take action. Having a clear target to work towards encourages disciplined saving, investing, and spending habits. It provides a sense of purpose and focus, making it easier to stay committed to financial plans even when faced with challenges or temptations.

Financial Planning: Financial goals serve as the foundation for developing a comprehensive financial plan. By identifying specific goals and the timeline for achieving them, individuals can create a roadmap for allocating resources, managing cash flow, and making strategic financial decisions. A well-crafted financial plan ensures that resources are directed towards achieving priorities in a systematic and efficient manner.

Measurement and Evaluation: Financial goals provide benchmarks for measuring progress and evaluating financial performance over time. Regularly tracking progress towards goals allows individuals to assess whether they are on track to meet objectives or if adjustments need to be made to their financial plan. This ongoing evaluation process helps to identify areas of strength and areas that require improvement, enabling more effective financial management.

Sense of Accomplishment: Achieving financial goals provides a sense of accomplishment and satisfaction. Whether it's reaching a milestone such as paying off a loan or reaching a savings target, meeting financial goals reinforces positive financial behaviors and builds confidence in one's ability to manage money effectively. Celebrating achievements along the way helps to maintain motivation and momentum towards future goals.

Long-Term Financial Security and Well-Being: Ultimately, setting and achieving financial goals is essential for long-term financial security and well-being. By aligning financial decisions with personal values and aspirations, individuals can create a more fulfilling and secure financial future for themselves and their families. Whether it's building wealth, reducing financial stress, or achieving financial independence, setting clear financial goals is the first step towards realizing these objectives.

In summary, setting financial goals is vital for providing direction, motivation, and focus in managing personal or organizational finances. By establishing clear objectives, developing a plan to achieve them, and regularly monitoring progress, individuals can take control of their financial future and work towards greater financial security, success, and well-being.

Differentiating between needs and wants

Differentiating between needs and wants is essential for effective financial management and budgeting. Here's a breakdown of the key differences between needs and wants:

Needs:

Essential for Survival: Needs are items or expenses that are necessary for basic survival and well-being. These are things that individuals require to maintain their health, safety, and basic living standards.

Non-Discretionary: Needs are often non-discretionary, meaning they are unavoidable expenses that individuals must meet to sustain their lives and meet their fundamental needs.

Examples: Examples of needs include food, shelter, clothing, healthcare, utilities (such as water, electricity, heating), transportation (for work or essential travel), and basic hygiene products.

Wants:

Desires or Preferences: Wants are items or expenses that are desired or preferred by individuals, but they are not essential for survival or basic well-being. Wants are often driven by personal preferences, lifestyle choices, or desires for comfort and enjoyment.

Discretionary: Wants are discretionary expenses, meaning they are optional and can be foregone or delayed without significantly impacting an individual's basic needs or well-being.

Examples: Examples of wants include luxury items, entertainment (such as dining out, going to movies or concerts), travel for leisure, hobbies, fashion accessories, electronics (beyond basic necessities), and other non-essential goods or services.

Key considerations for distinguishing between needs and wants:

Priority: Needs should always take precedence over wants when allocating financial resources. Ensuring that essential needs are met should be the primary focus of budgeting and financial planning.

Budgeting: It's important to budget and allocate funds first to cover necessary needs before considering discretionary wants. By prioritizing needs in budgeting, individuals can ensure financial stability and avoid overspending on non-essential items.

Critical Thinking: Practicing critical thinking and discernment is essential for distinguishing between needs and wants. It involves evaluating whether an expense is truly necessary for survival and well-being or if it's driven by wants or desires.

Flexibility: While needs are essential, wants can vary based on individual preferences, values, and lifestyle choices. It's important to recognize that what constitutes a want for one person may be a need for another. Budgeting allows individuals to make conscious choices about how they allocate their financial resources based on their unique circumstances and priorities.

By understanding the difference between needs and wants, individuals can make informed financial decisions, prioritize spending based on essential needs, and align their financial resources with their values and goals.

This helps promote responsible money management, avoid unnecessary debt, and work towards long-term financial stability and well-being.

Creating a budgeting mindset

Developing a budgeting mindset is essential for effectively managing personal finances and achieving financial goals. Here are some key steps to cultivate a budgeting mindset:

Set Clear Financial Goals: Start by defining specific, measurable, achievable, relevant, and time-bound (SMART) financial goals. Whether it's paying off debt, saving for a down payment on a house, or building an emergency fund, having clear objectives provides motivation and direction for budgeting efforts.

Track Income and Expenses: Get into the habit of tracking income and expenses regularly. This could involve keeping receipts, using budgeting apps, or maintaining a spreadsheet to monitor where money is coming from and where it's going. Understanding cash flow is fundamental to effective budgeting.

Differentiate Between Needs and Wants: Practice distinguishing between essential needs and discretionary wants. Prioritize spending on needs such as housing, food, and healthcare, and be mindful of unnecessary expenses that can be reduced or eliminated.

Create a Realistic Budget: Develop a realistic budget that aligns with your financial goals and priorities. Allocate income to cover essential needs first, then allocate funds for savings, debt repayment, and discretionary spending. Be honest with yourself about your income and expenses to ensure your budget is achievable.

Embrace Frugality and Resourcefulness: Cultivate a mindset of frugality and resourcefulness. Look for opportunities to save money through cost-cutting measures, comparison shopping, using coupons or discounts, and finding creative ways to stretch your dollars further.

Practice Discipline and Self-Control: Budgeting requires discipline and self-control to stick to your financial plan, even when faced with temptations to overspend or indulge in impulse purchases. Set boundaries for discretionary spending and avoid making impulsive financial decisions that derail your budgeting efforts.

Stay Flexible and Adapt: Recognize that life is unpredictable, and financial circumstances may change. Stay flexible and be prepared to adjust your budget as needed in response to changes in income, expenses, or financial goals. Adaptability is key to maintaining a sustainable budgeting mindset over the long term.

Celebrate Progress and Milestones: Celebrate achievements and milestones along the way to keep yourself motivated and engaged with your budgeting journey. Whether it's reaching a savings goal, paying off a debt, or sticking to your budget for a consecutive month, acknowledge your successes and use them as fuel to propel you forward.

Seek Support and Accountability: Surround yourself with a supportive network of friends, family, or financial advisors who can provide encouragement, accountability, and guidance on your budgeting journey. Share your goals and progress with others to stay motivated and accountable.

Focus on Long-Term Financial Well-Being: Keep your focus on the big picture of long-term financial well-being and security. Remember that budgeting is not just about managing money in the present but also about building a solid foundation for your future financial success and peace of mind.

By adopting a budgeting mindset and implementing these strategies, you can take control of your finances, make informed financial decisions, and work towards achieving your financial goals with confidence and purpose.

3

Assessing Your Financial Situation

Conducting a financial inventory

Conducting a financial inventory involves thoroughly assessing your current financial situation by compiling detailed information about your assets, liabilities, income, and expenses. Here's how to conduct a financial inventory:

Gather Financial Documents: Collect all relevant financial documents, including bank statements, investment account statements, credit card statements, loan statements, tax returns, pay stubs, and any other records related to your finances.

List Your Assets:

Identify and list all of your assets, including:

- Cash and savings accounts

- Checking accounts
- Investment accounts (e.g., retirement accounts, brokerage accounts)
- Real estate properties (e.g., primary residence, rental properties)
- Vehicles
- Personal property of significant value (e.g., jewelry, collectibles)
- Record the current market value or estimated worth of each asset.

Calculate Your Liabilities:

Identify and list all of your liabilities, including:

- Mortgage(s)
- Auto loans
- Student loans
- Credit card debt
- Personal loans
- Other outstanding debts
- Record the outstanding balance, interest rate, and minimum monthly payment for each liability.

Assess Your Income:

Determine your total monthly income from all sources, including:

- Salary or wages
- Bonuses or commissions
- Rental income

- Investment income (e.g., dividends, interest)
- Side hustles or freelance work
- Calculate your net income after taxes and deductions.

Track Your Expenses:

- Review your bank and credit card statements to identify and categorize your expenses over the past few months.
- Categorize expenses into fixed expenses (e.g., rent/mortgage, utilities, insurance) and variable expenses (e.g., groceries, dining out, entertainment).
- Calculate your average monthly expenses for each category.

Calculate Your Net Worth:

- Subtract your total liabilities from your total assets to calculate your net worth.
- Your net worth provides a snapshot of your overall financial health and indicates whether your assets exceed your liabilities.

Analyze Your Financial Situation:

- Review your financial inventory to assess your current financial situation objectively.
- Identify areas of strength (e.g., high savings rate, low debt) and areas

for improvement (e.g., excessive spending, high-interest debt).
- Consider your short-term and long-term financial goals and how your current financial situation aligns with them.

Identify Opportunities for Improvement:

- Based on your analysis, identify specific actions you can take to improve your financial health, such as reducing expenses, paying down debt, increasing savings, or investing for the future.
- Set priorities and develop a plan of action to address any areas of concern or opportunities for improvement.

Review and Update Regularly:

- Conduct regular reviews of your financial inventory to track progress, update information, and adjust your financial plan as needed.
- Regular monitoring ensures that you stay informed about your financial status and can make informed decisions to achieve your financial goals.

By conducting a thorough financial inventory, you gain a comprehensive understanding of your current financial situation, which serves as the foundation for effective financial planning and decision-making.

It enables you to identify opportunities for improvement, set realistic financial goals, and take proactive steps to enhance your financial well-being.

Tracking income and expenses

Tracking income and expenses is a fundamental aspect of personal financial management. Here's how to effectively track your income and expenses:

Choose a Tracking Method: Select a method for tracking your income and expenses that works best for you. Options include:

- Pen and paper: Keep a notebook or ledger to manually record all income and expenses.
- Spreadsheet: Create a spreadsheet using software like Microsoft Excel or Google Sheets to input and categorize income and expenses.
- Budgeting apps: Utilize budgeting apps such as Mint, YNAB (You Need a Budget), or Personal Capital, which automate the process and provide additional features like categorization, spending insights, and goal tracking.

Record Income Sources: Start by recording all sources of income, including:

- Salary or wages from employment
- Bonuses or commissions

- Rental income
- Investment income (e.g., dividends, interest)
- Side hustle or freelance income
- Any other sources of revenue

Categorize Expenses: Categorize your expenses into specific categories to better understand where your money is going. Common expense categories include:

- Housing (rent/mortgage, utilities, property taxes)
- Transportation (car payments, gas, maintenance, public transportation)
- Food (groceries, dining out)
- Insurance (health, auto, homeowners/renters)
- Debt payments (credit cards, loans)
- Entertainment (movies, dining out, hobbies)
- Personal care (healthcare, grooming)
- Savings and investments
- Miscellaneous expenses

Record Every Transaction: Consistently record every income and expense transaction as they occur. Include details such as the date, amount, description, and category. Be diligent about tracking even small expenses, as they can add up over time.

Regularly Review and Update: Set aside time on a regular basis (e.g., weekly, biweekly, monthly) to review and update your income and expense records. This helps ensure accuracy and provides insight into your spending habits and patterns.

Use Tools and Automation: Take advantage of tools and automation to simplify the tracking process. Budgeting apps can automatically categorize transactions, provide spending insights, and generate reports, making it easier to manage your finances efficiently.

Analyze Spending Patterns: Periodically analyze your spending patterns to identify areas where you may be overspending or where there may be opportunities to save. Look for trends, outliers, and areas where adjustments can be made to align with your financial goals.

Set Budgets and Goals: Use the insights gained from tracking your income and expenses to establish budgets and financial goals. Set realistic targets for each expense category and track your progress over time. Adjust budgets and goals as needed based on changes in income, expenses, or financial priorities.

Monitor Your Financial Health: Regularly monitor your financial health by comparing your actual income and expenses against your budgeted amounts and financial goals. This helps you stay on track, make informed financial decisions, and work towards achieving your desired financial outcomes.

By diligently tracking your income and expenses, you gain visibility into your financial habits, make more informed decisions, and ultimately improve your financial well-being.

Consistency and accuracy are key to effective tracking, so make it a habit to record transactions regularly and review your finances periodically.

Analyzing spending patterns

Analyzing spending patterns is a critical step in understanding how you manage your money and identifying areas where you can make improvements. Here's how to effectively analyze your spending patterns:

Gather Data: Collect all your financial records, including bank statements, credit card statements, receipts, and any other documents that detail your spending over a specific period. Make sure you have a comprehensive overview of your transactions.

Categorize Expenses: Organize your expenses into categories to better understand your spending habits. Common categories include housing, transportation, groceries, dining out, entertainment, utilities, healthcare, debt payments, savings, and miscellaneous expenses.

Use Technology: Consider leveraging personal finance tools or apps that automatically categorize your transactions. This can save time and provide more accurate insights into your spending patterns. Many apps also offer visualization tools like charts and graphs to help you analyze your data more effectively.

Identify Trends: Look for trends or patterns in your spending habits. Are there certain categories where you consistently overspend? Are there specific months or periods when your spending tends to increase? Identifying trends can help you pinpoint areas for improvement.

Assess Variability: Evaluate the variability of your spending across different categories. Some expenses, like rent or mortgage payments, may be fixed and consistent each month, while others, like dining out or entertainment, may vary more from month to month. Understanding variability can help you better anticipate and plan for future expenses.

Compare Actual vs. Budgeted: Compare your actual spending against your budget or financial goals. Are you staying within your budgeted limits for each category? If not, why? Identifying discrepancies between your actual and planned spending can highlight areas where you may need to adjust your budget or spending habits.

Identify Problem Areas: Pinpoint areas of excessive or unnecessary spending. Are there expenses that don't align with your financial priorities or values? Are there recurring subscriptions or memberships that you no longer use or need? Identifying problem areas can help you make more informed decisions about where to cut back.

Set Priorities: Determine which expenses are essential and which ones are discretionary. Prioritize spending on needs over wants, and allocate your resources accordingly. Focus on trimming expenses in non-essential categories to free up more money for savings, debt repayment, or other financial goals.

Create Actionable Goals: Based on your analysis, create actionable goals to improve your spending habits. Set specific targets for reducing spending in problem areas, increasing savings rates, paying off debt, or achieving other financial objectives. Break down larger goals into smaller, manageable steps to make progress more achievable.

Track Progress: Continuously monitor your spending patterns and track your progress toward your goals over time. Regularly revisit your budget and adjust as needed based on changes in your financial circumstances or priorities. Celebrate milestones and achievements along the way to stay motivated.

By analyzing your spending patterns regularly, you gain valuable insights into your financial behavior and can make more informed decisions to improve your financial well-being. It's an essential step in taking control of your finances and working toward your long-term financial goals.

Identifying areas for improvement

Identifying areas for improvement in your finances involves assessing your current financial situation and pinpointing areas where you can make changes to better align with your financial goals. Here's how to identify areas for improvement:

Review Your Financial Goals: Start by revisiting your financial goals. What are you trying to achieve? Whether it's paying off debt, saving for a down payment on a house, or building an emergency fund, your goals provide a roadmap for identifying areas where you need to improve your financial habits.

Conduct a Financial Inventory: Take stock of your income, expenses, assets, and liabilities. Review your bank statements, credit card statements, and other financial records to understand where your money is coming from and where it's going. This will help you identify areas where you may be overspending or where you could be allocating more resources to achieve your goals.

Analyze Your Spending Patterns: Examine your spending habits to identify areas for improvement. Look for patterns of excessive or unnecessary spending, recurring expenses that can be reduced or eliminated, and opportunities to reallocate funds to higher-priority areas.

Assess Debt Levels: Evaluate your current debt levels and interest rates. Are you carrying high-interest debt that is eating into your budget? Consider strategies for paying down debt more aggressively, such as consolidating high-interest debt, refinancing loans, or negotiating lower interest rates.

Review Fixed Expenses: Take a close look at your fixed expenses, such as rent or mortgage payments, utilities, insurance premiums, and subscription services. Are there opportunities to reduce these costs through negotiation, refinancing, or switching to more cost-effective alternatives?

Evaluate Variable Expenses: Examine your variable expenses, such as groceries, dining out, entertainment, and discretionary purchases. Are there areas where you're consistently overspending? Look for opportunities to cut back on non-essential expenses and reallocate those funds toward your financial goals.

Assess Savings and Investments: Review your savings and investment accounts to ensure you're maximizing opportunities for growth and compounding. Are you saving enough for retirement? Do you have an adequate emergency fund? Consider automating savings contributions to ensure consistent progress toward your savings goals.

Evaluate Income Opportunities: Explore opportunities to increase your income through additional sources of revenue, such as side hustles, freelance work, or passive income streams. Increasing your income can provide more financial flexibility and accelerate progress toward your goals.

Consider Lifestyle Adjustments: Evaluate your lifestyle and consider whether there are adjustments you can make to better align with your financial priorities. This could involve downsizing your living space, cutting back on discretionary expenses, or adopting a more minimalist approach to consumption.

Set Priorities and Action Steps: Based on your assessment, prioritize areas for improvement and develop actionable steps to address them. Set specific, measurable goals and timelines for achieving them. Break larger goals down into smaller, more manageable tasks to make progress more achievable.

By identifying areas for improvement in your finances and taking proactive steps to address them, you can make meaningful progress toward your financial goals and achieve greater financial stability and security over time.

Regularly revisit your financial plan and adjust as needed to stay on track toward long-term financial success.

4

Building a Solid Budget

Establishing short-term and long-term financial goals

Establishing both short-term and long-term financial goals is crucial for creating a roadmap to achieve financial success. Here's how to establish and differentiate between these two types of goals:

Short-Term Financial Goals:

Definition: Short-term financial goals are objectives that you aim to achieve within the near future, typically within the next 1-3 years.

Examples:

- Building an emergency fund to cover 3-6 months' worth of living expenses.
- Paying off high-interest credit card debt within the next 12 months.

- Saving for a vacation or holiday within the next year.
- Investing in continuing education or professional development courses to enhance skills and career prospects.
- Saving for a down payment on a car or home purchase within the next 2 years.

Characteristics:

- Short-term goals are typically specific, measurable, and time-bound (SMART).
- They often involve relatively smaller amounts of money and shorter timeframes compared to long-term goals.
- Short-term goals may serve as stepping stones toward achieving larger, long-term objectives.
- They are essential for building financial momentum and establishing good financial habits.

Long-Term Financial Goals:

Definition: Long-term financial goals are objectives that you aim to achieve over an extended period, typically spanning 5 years or more.

Examples:

- Saving for retirement and achieving financial independence by a certain age.
- Paying off a mortgage and owning a home outright within the next

15-30 years.
- Funding a child's college education or wedding expenses.
- Building a sizable investment portfolio to generate passive income in retirement.
- Establishing a legacy or charitable giving plan.

Characteristics:

- Long-term goals require careful planning, consistency, and discipline over an extended period.
- They often involve larger sums of money and significant life milestones or aspirations.
- Long-term goals may require investment strategies to grow wealth over time, such as retirement accounts, real estate investments, or diversified portfolios.
- They provide direction and purpose for your financial decisions and help ensure that you're working toward your desired future outcomes.

Differentiating Between Short-Term and Long-Term Goals:

Timeframe: Short-term goals are achievable within a relatively short timeframe (1-3 years), while long-term goals require more time and sustained effort (5 years or more).

Scope: Short-term goals tend to focus on immediate needs or desires, such as debt repayment, emergency savings, or specific purchases. Long-term goals encompass broader aspirations and major life milestones, such as retirement, homeownership, or financial independence.

Priority: Short-term goals may take precedence over long-term goals in certain situations, especially if they involve urgent financial needs or high-interest debt. However, both short-term and long-term goals are essential for comprehensive financial planning and should be prioritized accordingly.

Establishing a mix of short-term and long-term financial goals allows you to balance immediate needs with future aspirations and create a well-rounded financial plan.

Regularly review and update your goals as your financial situation evolves, and celebrate milestones along the way to stay motivated and on track toward achieving financial success.

Creating a realistic budget plan

Creating a realistic budget plan involves assessing your financial situation, setting achievable goals, and allocating your income effectively to cover expenses, savings, and debt payments. Here's a step-by-step guide to creating a realistic budget plan:

Assess Your Financial Situation:

- Gather information about your income, expenses, assets, and debts.
- Calculate your total monthly income from all sources.
- Determine your fixed expenses (e.g., rent/mortgage, utilities, insurance) and variable expenses (e.g., groceries, dining out, entertain-

ment).

- Identify any outstanding debts, including credit card balances, loans, and other liabilities.
- Calculate your net worth by subtracting your total liabilities from your total assets.

Set Financial Goals:

- Define your short-term and long-term financial goals based on your priorities and aspirations.
- Make sure your goals are specific, measurable, achievable, relevant, and time-bound (SMART).
- Examples of financial goals include building an emergency fund, paying off debt, saving for a down payment on a house, or funding retirement.

Determine Your Budget Categories:

- Divide your expenses into categories to better organize your budget.
- Common budget categories include housing, transportation, groceries, utilities, healthcare, debt payments, savings, and discretionary spending.
- Allocate funds to each category based on your spending habits and financial goals.

Estimate Your Expenses:

- Review your past spending habits to estimate your monthly expenses in each category.
- Be realistic about your spending patterns and account for irregular or seasonal expenses.

Calculate Your Disposable Income:

- Subtract your total estimated expenses from your total monthly income to determine your disposable income.
- Your disposable income is the amount of money you have left over after covering all essential expenses and debt payments.

Adjust Your Budget as Needed:

- If your estimated expenses exceed your income, look for areas where you can cut back or reduce spending.
- Consider negotiating lower bills, switching to more affordable alternatives, or eliminating non-essential expenses.
- Prioritize your spending based on your financial goals and values.

Allocate Funds for Savings and Debt Repayment:

- Allocate a portion of your disposable income towards savings and debt repayment.
- Aim to save at least 10-20% of your income for short-term and long-term goals, including emergency savings, retirement, and other financial objectives.
- Allocate additional funds towards debt repayment to accelerate progress and reduce interest costs.

Monitor Your Budget Regularly:

- Track your actual spending against your budget on a regular basis.
- Review your budget monthly or quarterly to ensure you're staying on track and making progress towards your financial goals.
- Make adjustments as needed to accommodate changes in income, expenses, or financial priorities.

Celebrate Milestones and Adjustments:

- Celebrate your achievements and milestones along the way to stay motivated.
- Be flexible and willing to adjust your budget as needed to reflect changes in your financial situation or goals.
- Remember that budgeting is a dynamic process, and it's okay to make changes as your circumstances evolve.

Seek Support and Accountability:

- Consider enlisting the support of a financial advisor, friend, or family member to help you stay accountable to your budget and financial goals.
- Share your progress and challenges with others to stay motivated and receive feedback and support.

Creating a realistic budget plan requires careful consideration of your financial situation, goals, and priorities.

By following these steps and regularly reviewing and adjusting your budget, you can effectively manage your finances and work towards achieving your financial goals.

Allocating income to various expense categories (housing, food, transportation, etc.)

Allocating income to various expense categories is a crucial aspect of creating a budget that reflects your financial priorities and helps you manage your money effectively.

Here's a step-by-step guide to allocating your income to different expense categories:

Calculate Your Total Monthly Income:

Determine your total monthly income from all sources, including salaries, wages, bonuses, commissions, rental income, investment income, and any other sources of revenue.

Determine Your Fixed Expenses:

- Identify your fixed expenses, which are recurring costs that remain relatively stable from month to month.
- Common fixed expenses include:

1. <u>Housing:</u> Rent or mortgage payments, property taxes, homeowner's insurance, and maintenance costs.
2. <u>Utilities:</u> Electricity, water, gas, internet, cable, and phone bills.
3. <u>Insurance:</u> Health insurance, auto insurance, life insurance, and other insurance premiums.
4. <u>Debt Payments:</u> Minimum payments on loans, credit cards, or other debts.

- Total the monthly cost of your fixed expenses.

Estimate Your Variable Expenses:

- Variable expenses are costs that can fluctuate from month to month based on your consumption or usage.
- Common variable expenses include:

1. <u>Food:</u> Groceries, dining out, and snacks.
2. Transportation: Gasoline, public transportation fares, vehicle maintenance, and parking fees.
3. <u>Personal Care:</u> Toiletries, grooming products, and haircuts.
4. <u>Entertainment:</u> Movies, concerts, dining out, hobbies, and subscriptions.
5. <u>Miscellaneous:</u> Gifts, clothing, household supplies, and other discretionary purchases.

- Estimate your monthly spending in each variable expense category based on past spending habits or industry benchmarks.

Allocate Funds for Savings and Investments:

- Allocate a portion of your income towards savings and investments to achieve your financial goals.
- Common savings goals include emergency savings, retirement contributions, saving for a down payment on a house, or funding education expenses.
- Aim to save at least 10-20% of your income for savings and investments, but adjust based on your financial priorities and goals.

Consider Other Financial Priorities:

- Factor in any other financial priorities or obligations you may have, such as child support payments, alimony, or contributions to charitable organizations.
- Allocate funds accordingly to ensure you're meeting all your financial obligations.

Review Your Budget and Adjust as Needed:

- Total the allocated amounts for each expense category to ensure they do not exceed your total monthly income.

- If your allocated expenses exceed your income, review your budget to identify areas where you can cut back or reduce spending.
- Be realistic about your budget and prioritize essential expenses while making room for discretionary spending on non-essential items.

Monitor Your Spending and Adjustments:

- Track your actual spending against your budget each month to ensure you're staying on track.
- Make adjustments to your budget as needed to reflect changes in your financial situation, income, expenses, or priorities.
- Regularly review and update your budget to ensure it remains relevant and effective in helping you achieve your financial goals.

By allocating your income to various expense categories in a structured manner, you can create a balanced budget that aligns with your financial goals and priorities.

Regularly monitoring and adjusting your budget allows you to stay on top of your finances and make informed decisions to achieve financial stability and success.

Setting aside funds for savings and emergencies

Setting aside funds for savings and emergencies is a critical component of a healthy financial plan. Here's how to effectively allocate funds for these purposes:

Establish Emergency Savings:

- Aim to build an emergency fund to cover unexpected expenses or financial emergencies, such as medical bills, car repairs, or job loss.
- Start by setting a goal to save 3-6 months' worth of living expenses. If you have dependents or work in an unstable industry, consider saving even more.
- Calculate your monthly living expenses, including housing, utilities, groceries, transportation, insurance, debt payments, and other essentials.
- Open a separate, easily accessible savings account specifically designated for your emergency fund.
- Set up automatic transfers from your checking account to your emergency fund savings account each month to ensure consistent contributions.
- Treat your emergency fund as a financial priority, and avoid dipping into it for non-urgent expenses.

Allocate Funds for Short-Term Savings Goals:

- Identify short-term financial goals that you want to achieve within the next 1-3 years, such as saving for a vacation, a new vehicle, or a home down payment.
- Determine the total amount you need to save for each short-term goal and the timeframe in which you want to achieve it.
- Divide the total amount by the number of months until your target

date to calculate the monthly savings needed to reach each goal.

- Open separate savings accounts or designate sub-accounts within your existing savings account for each short-term savings goal.
- Set up automatic transfers from your checking account to each short-term savings account to ensure you're making progress towards your goals consistently.

Prioritize Long-Term Savings Goals:

- Identify long-term financial goals, such as retirement savings, purchasing a home, funding education expenses, or building wealth.
- Determine the total amount you need to save for each long-term goal and the timeframe over which you plan to achieve it.
- Calculate the monthly contributions needed to reach each long-term savings goal based on your target date and expected rate of return.
- Contribute to tax-advantaged retirement accounts, such as 401(k)s, IRAs, or employer-sponsored retirement plans, to maximize tax benefits and long-term growth potential.
- Consider diversifying your long-term savings across different investment vehicles, such as stocks, bonds, mutual funds, or real estate, to mitigate risk and maximize returns over time.
- Review your progress towards your long-term savings goals regularly and adjust your contributions as needed based on changes in your financial situation or investment performance.

Maintain Discipline and Consistency:

- Make saving a habit by prioritizing it in your budget and treating it as a non-negotiable expense.
- Resist the temptation to spend your savings on non-essential purchases or lifestyle upgrades.
- Stay disciplined and consistent with your savings contributions, even during periods of financial uncertainty or market volatility.
- Celebrate milestones along the way to stay motivated and reinforce positive saving habits.

By setting aside funds for savings and emergencies, you can build a financial safety net, achieve your short-term and long-term financial goals, and enhance your overall financial well-being.

Regular contributions to your savings accounts ensure that you're prepared for unexpected expenses and have a solid foundation for future financial success.

5

Implementing Effective Budgeting Strategies

Using budgeting tools and apps

Budgeting tools and apps can be valuable resources for managing your finances effectively, tracking expenses, and achieving your financial goals.

Here's how to use budgeting tools and apps to streamline your budgeting process:

Choose the Right Tool or App:

- Research and explore different budgeting tools and apps available to find one that best suits your needs, preferences, and financial goals.
- Consider factors such as user interface, features, compatibility with your devices, security measures, and cost (if applicable).

Set Up Your Budget:

- Once you've chosen a budgeting tool or app, set up your budget by inputting your income, expenses, savings goals, and other financial information.
- Customize your budget categories to align with your spending habits and priorities, and establish budget limits for each category.

Link Your Accounts:

- Many budgeting tools and apps allow you to link your bank accounts, credit cards, investment accounts, and other financial accounts.
- Linking your accounts enables the app to automatically import and categorize your transactions, saving you time and effort in manual data entry.

Track Your Spending:

- Regularly monitor your spending by reviewing your transactions within the budgeting tool or app.
- Categorize each transaction accurately to gain insights into your spending habits and identify areas where you can cut back or reallocate funds.

Set Savings Goals:

- Utilize the goal-setting features of the budgeting tool or app to establish savings goals for short-term and long-term objectives.
- Set specific targets, timelines, and amounts for each savings goal, such as building an emergency fund, saving for a vacation, or funding retirement.

Receive Alerts and Notifications:

- Take advantage of alerts and notifications provided by the budgeting tool or app to stay informed about your financial progress and upcoming expenses.
- Set up alerts for overspending, upcoming bill due dates, low account balances, or when you've reached a savings milestone.

Use Budgeting Features and Tools:

- Explore the various budgeting features and tools offered by the app to enhance your financial management.
- Some common features include expense tracking, budgeting templates, goal trackers, spending analysis reports, bill reminders, and debt payoff calculators.

Review and Adjust Regularly:

- Regularly review your budget and spending patterns within the app to ensure you're staying on track with your financial goals.
- Make adjustments to your budget as needed based on changes in your income, expenses, financial priorities, or unexpected events.

Take Advantage of Support and Resources:

- Many budgeting tools and apps offer educational resources, tutorials, and customer support to help you maximize the benefits of the app and improve your financial literacy.
- Explore these resources to learn more about budgeting best practices, money management tips, and strategies for achieving financial success.

Protect Your Information:

- Be mindful of security measures and privacy settings within the budgeting tool or app to safeguard your financial information.
- Use strong, unique passwords, enable multi-factor authentication (if available), and review the app's privacy policy to understand how your data is handled and protected.

By leveraging budgeting tools and apps effectively, you can gain greater control over your finances, track your progress towards your financial goals, and make informed decisions to improve your financial well-being.

Regularly using these tools can help you develop healthy financial habits and achieve long-term financial success.

Tips for managing irregular income

Managing irregular income can present unique challenges compared to a consistent salary or wage. However, with proper planning and strategies, you can effectively manage fluctuations in your income and maintain financial stability.

Here are some tips for managing irregular income:

Create a Budget Based on Minimum Income:

- Estimate your average monthly income based on your lowest-earning months or a conservative estimate of your expected income.
- Build your budget around this minimum income to ensure you can cover essential expenses during periods of lower earnings.

Prioritize Essential Expenses:

- Identify your non-negotiable expenses, such as housing, utilities, groceries, insurance premiums, and debt payments.
- Allocate a portion of your income to cover these essential expenses first to ensure your basic needs are met regardless of fluctuations in income.

Build an Emergency Fund:

- Establish an emergency fund to cover unexpected expenses or income gaps during lean months.
- Aim to save 3-6 months' worth of living expenses in your emergency fund to provide a financial cushion during periods of irregular income.

Track Your Cash Flow:

- Monitor your income and expenses closely to track your cash flow and identify patterns in your earning and spending habits.
- Use budgeting tools or apps to categorize your transactions and gain insights into your financial behavior.

Create a Buffer with Variable Income:

- Set aside a portion of your higher-earning months to create a buffer or reserve fund to smooth out income fluctuations.
- Use surplus income from peak months to cover expenses during slower months, helping to maintain consistency in your finances.

Diversify Income Sources:

- Explore opportunities to diversify your income sources to reduce reliance on a single stream of income.
- Consider taking on freelance work, consulting gigs, part-time jobs, or passive income streams to supplement your primary income and increase overall financial stability.

Adjust Spending During Peak Months:

- During months with higher income, resist the temptation to overspend and instead allocate surplus funds strategically.
- Use extra income to pay down debt, build savings, invest for the future, or fund long-term financial goals.

Set Realistic Financial Goals:

- Establish realistic financial goals that take into account your irregular income and fluctuating financial circumstances.
- Break down larger goals into smaller, manageable milestones that you can work towards consistently, regardless of variations in income.

Maintain Flexibility and Adaptability:

- Stay flexible and adaptable in your financial planning to accommodate changes in your income or expenses.

- Be prepared to adjust your budget, savings goals, and spending habits as needed to reflect fluctuations in your income and financial priorities.

Seek Professional Advice if Needed:

- Consider consulting with a financial advisor or planner who can provide personalized guidance and strategies for managing irregular income.
- An advisor can help you develop a customized financial plan tailored to your unique financial situation, goals, and risk tolerance.

Managing irregular income requires proactive planning, discipline, and flexibility.

By implementing these tips and strategies, you can navigate fluctuations in your income more effectively and achieve greater financial stability over time.

Strategies for reducing expenses

Reducing expenses is a key strategy for improving your financial health and achieving your financial goals. Here are some effective strategies for cutting costs and minimizing expenses:

Track Your Spending:

- Start by tracking your expenses to understand where your money is going.
- Use budgeting tools or apps to categorize your expenses and identify areas where you can cut back.

Create a Budget:

- Establish a budget that outlines your income and expenses.
- Allocate funds to essential categories such as housing, utilities, groceries, transportation, and debt payments.
- Set limits for discretionary spending on non-essential items like dining out, entertainment, and shopping.

Negotiate Bills and Expenses:

- Negotiate with service providers such as cable companies, internet providers, and insurance companies to lower your bills.
- Ask for discounts, promotions, or loyalty rewards, or consider switching to cheaper alternatives.

Reduce Housing Costs:

- Consider downsizing to a smaller, more affordable home or apartment.
- Explore options for refinancing your mortgage to secure a lower

interest rate and reduce monthly payments.

- Rent out a spare room or consider house hacking to generate additional income.

Cut Transportation Costs:

- Use public transportation, carpooling, or biking instead of driving to save on gas and maintenance costs.
- Downsize to a more fuel-efficient vehicle or consider leasing instead of buying to lower monthly payments.
- Avoid unnecessary trips and consolidate errands to minimize mileage and reduce expenses.

Save on Food Expenses:

- Plan meals in advance and create a grocery list to avoid impulse purchases.
- Buy generic brands instead of name brands to save on groceries.
- Cook meals at home instead of dining out, and pack lunches for work or school to save money.

Slash Entertainment Expenses:

- Cancel subscriptions and memberships for services you don't use or need.

- Look for free or low-cost entertainment options such as community events, parks, and libraries.
- Limit dining out and choose budget-friendly alternatives like picnics or potluck dinners with friends.

Reduce Utility Bills:

- Turn off lights, appliances, and electronics when not in use to lower electricity costs.
- Install energy-efficient light bulbs, appliances, and fixtures to save on utilities.
- Adjust thermostats and use programmable thermostats to regulate heating and cooling expenses.

Cut Credit Card Debt:

- Pay off high-interest credit card debt as quickly as possible to avoid accruing interest charges.
- Consolidate debt with a balance transfer or consider debt consolidation to lower interest rates and simplify payments.
- Avoid using credit cards for unnecessary purchases and focus on paying down existing balances.

Review Insurance Policies:

- Shop around for insurance policies to find the best rates and coverage options.
- Consider bundling policies with the same insurer for discounts on premiums.
- Review your coverage limits and deductibles to ensure you're not overpaying for unnecessary coverage.

Automate Savings:

- Set up automatic transfers from your checking account to a savings or investment account to ensure consistent savings.
- Treat savings as a non-negotiable expense and prioritize it in your budget to build a financial cushion for emergencies and future goals.

By implementing these strategies and making conscious choices to reduce expenses, you can free up more money to save, invest, and achieve your financial objectives.

Start by identifying areas where you can cut back and gradually implement changes to improve your financial well-being over time.

Techniques for increasing income

Increasing income is a key strategy for improving your financial situation and achieving your financial goals. Here are some effective techniques for boosting your income:

Negotiate a Raise or Promotion:

- Advocate for yourself and present a strong case for why you deserve a raise or promotion based on your contributions, skills, and achievements.
- Highlight your accomplishments, skills, and value to the company during performance reviews or salary negotiations.

Seek Additional Employment Opportunities:

- Take on a part-time job, freelance work, or side hustle to supplement your primary income.
- Look for flexible opportunities that allow you to work around your schedule and interests, such as remote work, consulting, or gig economy jobs.

Upgrade Your Skills and Education:

- Invest in ongoing education, training, or certification programs to improve your skills and qualifications.
- Consider pursuing advanced degrees, professional certifications, or specialized training in high-demand fields to increase your earning potential.

Start a Business or Entrepreneurial Venture:

- Launch a small business or entrepreneurial venture based on your expertise, interests, or passions.
- Identify niche markets or unmet needs and develop products or services that provide value to customers.
- Utilize online platforms and marketplaces to reach a wider audience and grow your business.

Monetize Your Hobbies and Talents:

- Explore opportunities to monetize your hobbies, talents, or creative skills.
- Consider selling handmade crafts, artwork, photography, or digital products online through e-commerce platforms or marketplaces.

Rent Out Assets or Property:

- Rent out unused space in your home or property through platforms like Airbnb or VRBO.
- Lease out equipment, vehicles, or other assets to generate rental income.

Invest in Real Estate:

- Invest in income-producing real estate properties such as rental properties, vacation rentals, or commercial real estate.

- Consider real estate crowdfunding platforms or real estate investment trusts (REITs) for passive real estate investing opportunities.

Generate Passive Income Streams:

- Create passive income streams by investing in dividend-paying stocks, bonds, mutual funds, or exchange-traded funds (ETFs).
- Build a portfolio of income-producing assets such as rental properties, dividend-paying stocks, peer-to-peer lending, or royalties from intellectual property.

Explore Affiliate Marketing or Referral Programs:

- Partner with companies or brands as an affiliate marketer to earn commissions for promoting products or services.
- Participate in referral programs or affiliate networks to earn bonuses or incentives for referring customers or clients.

Provide Consulting or Coaching Services:

- Offer consulting, coaching, or advisory services based on your expertise, knowledge, or experience.
- Help individuals or businesses solve problems, achieve goals, or improve performance in specific areas.

Network and Build Relationships:

- Network with industry professionals, colleagues, and mentors to uncover new opportunities for career advancement, freelance work, or business partnerships.
- Attend industry events, conferences, and workshops to expand your professional network and stay informed about trends and opportunities in your field.

Invest in Yourself:

- Invest in personal development and self-improvement to enhance your skills, confidence, and mindset.
- Develop strong communication, leadership, and interpersonal skills that are valuable in any career or business endeavor.

By implementing these techniques and taking proactive steps to increase your income, you can create new opportunities for financial growth and achieve greater financial stability and success. Experiment with different strategies to find what works best for your unique circumstances, interests, and goals.

6

Overcoming Budgeting Challenges

Dealing with unexpected expenses

Dealing with unexpected expenses is a common challenge that can disrupt your financial plans and cause stress. Here are some strategies for handling unexpected expenses effectively:

Build an Emergency Fund:

- Establish an emergency fund specifically designated to cover unexpected expenses.
- Aim to save 3-6 months' worth of living expenses in your emergency fund to provide a financial cushion for unforeseen circumstances.

Prioritize Expenses:

- Assess the urgency and importance of the unexpected expense to determine how to address it.
- Prioritize essential expenses such as medical bills, car repairs, or home repairs that impact your safety, health, or well-being.

Review Your Budget:

- Review your budget to identify areas where you can temporarily reduce spending to free up funds for unexpected expenses.
- Cut back on discretionary expenses such as dining out, entertainment, or non-essential purchases until you've addressed the unexpected expense.

Explore Payment Options:

- Negotiate payment plans or installment agreements with creditors or service providers to spread out the cost of the unexpected expense over time.
- Inquire about hardship programs, financial assistance, or relief options available for specific types of expenses, such as medical bills or utility bills.

Use Available Resources:

- Tap into available resources such as savings, emergency funds, or other financial assets to cover the unexpected expense.

- Consider using low-interest credit cards, personal loans, or lines of credit as a temporary solution, but be mindful of interest charges and repayment terms.

Seek Additional Income:

- Explore opportunities to increase your income temporarily to cover unexpected expenses.
- Take on extra work, freelance projects, or part-time jobs to generate additional income to supplement your existing earnings.

Seek Financial Assistance:

- Research government programs, community resources, or charitable organizations that offer financial assistance or support for individuals facing unexpected expenses.
- Reach out to social services agencies, non-profit organizations, or religious institutions for guidance and support.

Avoid Borrowing Unnecessarily:

- Be cautious about borrowing money or taking on additional debt to cover unexpected expenses, especially if you're already struggling with debt.
- Evaluate the long-term impact of borrowing on your financial

situation and consider alternative solutions before taking on more debt.

Stay Calm and Positive:

- Remain calm and maintain a positive mindset when facing unexpected expenses.
- Focus on finding solutions and taking proactive steps to address the situation rather than dwelling on the problem.

Learn from the Experience:

- Use unexpected expenses as learning opportunities to improve your financial preparedness and resilience.
- Review your budget, emergency fund, and financial plan to identify areas for improvement and make adjustments to better handle future unexpected expenses.

By implementing these strategies and staying proactive in managing unexpected expenses, you can minimize their impact on your finances and maintain financial stability over the long term. Adjust your financial plan as needed to incorporate lessons learned from dealing with unexpected expenses and prioritize building a robust financial safety net to handle future challenges.

Addressing debt and managing credit

Addressing debt and managing credit are essential aspects of maintaining financial health and achieving long-term financial goals. Here are some strategies for effectively managing debt and credit:

Addressing Debt

Assess Your Debt Situation:

- Gather information about all your debts, including balances, interest rates, minimum payments, and due dates.
- Create a comprehensive list or spreadsheet to track your debts and understand the scope of your financial obligations.

Prioritize High-Interest Debt:

- Focus on paying off high-interest debts first, such as credit card balances or payday loans.
- Allocate extra funds towards these debts while making minimum payments on other debts to reduce interest costs and pay down balances faster.

Consider Debt Consolidation:

- Explore options for consolidating high-interest debts into a single, lower-interest loan or credit account.
- Consolidation methods include balance transfer credit cards, personal loans, or home equity loans, depending on your creditworthiness and financial situation.

Create a Repayment Plan:

- Develop a repayment plan that fits your budget and financial goals.
- Consider using the debt snowball or debt avalanche method to prioritize and pay off debts systematically.
- Set specific goals and milestones to track your progress and stay motivated throughout the debt repayment process.

Negotiate with Creditors:

- Contact creditors to negotiate lower interest rates, reduced payments, or alternative repayment plans if you're experiencing financial hardship.
- Be proactive and transparent about your situation, and provide documentation if necessary to support your request for assistance.

Avoid Taking on New Debt:

- Pause or minimize new borrowing while you focus on paying off existing debts.

- Resist the temptation to use credit cards or loans for non-essential purchases, and prioritize building a solid financial foundation before taking on additional debt.

Seek Professional Help if Needed:

- Consider working with a credit counseling agency or financial advisor specializing in debt management.
- A credit counselor can provide personalized guidance, negotiate with creditors on your behalf, and help you develop a sustainable plan to address your debt.

Managing Credit

Monitor Your Credit Report:

- Regularly review your credit report from all three major credit bureaus (Equifax, Experian, and TransUnion) to check for errors or fraudulent activity.
- Correct any inaccuracies promptly to ensure your credit report accurately reflects your financial history.

Maintain Good Payment Habits:

- Pay your bills on time every month to avoid late fees, penalties, and negative marks on your credit report.
- Set up automatic payments or reminders to ensure you never miss a payment deadline.

Manage Credit Card Usage:

- Use credit cards responsibly and avoid maxing out your credit limits.
- Keep credit card balances low relative to your credit limits to maintain a healthy credit utilization ratio, ideally below 30%.

Diversify Your Credit Mix:

- Maintain a diverse mix of credit accounts, including credit cards, installment loans, and mortgages, to demonstrate responsible credit management.
- Avoid opening multiple new credit accounts within a short period, as this can indicate financial instability and lower your credit score.

Limit Credit Inquiries:

- Minimize unnecessary credit inquiries, as each inquiry can temporarily lower your credit score.
- Only apply for new credit when necessary and research potential

lenders to find the best terms and rates before submitting applications.

Use Credit Wisely:

- Use credit as a tool to build and maintain financial stability, not as a means of financing a lifestyle beyond your means.
- Be mindful of the impact of credit decisions on your long-term financial health and make informed choices based on your goals and priorities.

Educate Yourself About Credit:

- Take advantage of educational resources and tools available to learn more about credit management, credit scores, and credit reporting.
- Stay informed about changes in credit laws, regulations, and industry practices to protect your rights as a consumer.

By addressing debt and managing credit responsibly, you can improve your financial well-being, build a positive credit history, and achieve your long-term financial goals.

Remember to stay proactive, informed, and disciplined in your approach to debt and credit management, and seek professional guidance if needed to navigate complex financial challenges effectively.

Handling financial setbacks and emergencies

Handling financial setbacks and emergencies requires a proactive approach and careful planning to mitigate their impact on your financial well-being. Here are some steps to effectively manage financial setbacks and emergencies:

1. Stay Calm and Assess the Situation:

- Take a deep breath and remain calm to think rationally and make informed decisions.
- Assess the nature and severity of the financial setback or emergency to understand the scope of the situation.

2. Build a Financial Safety Net:

- Establish an emergency fund to cover unexpected expenses or income disruptions.
- Aim to save 3-6 months' worth of living expenses in your emergency fund to provide a financial cushion for unforeseen circumstances.

3. Prioritize Essential Expenses:

- Identify and prioritize essential expenses such as housing, utilities, groceries, transportation, and insurance premiums.

- Allocate available funds towards essential expenses first to ensure your basic needs are met during the financial setback or emergency.

4. Review Your Budget and Cash Flow:

- Review your budget and cash flow to identify areas where you can temporarily reduce spending or reallocate funds to address the financial setback.
- Cut back on discretionary expenses such as dining out, entertainment, or non-essential purchases until you've stabilized your financial situation.

5. Communicate with Creditors and Service Providers:

- Contact creditors, lenders, landlords, and service providers to inform them of your situation and explore options for temporary relief or assistance.
- Negotiate payment plans, deferments, or hardship programs to spread out payments or reduce financial obligations during the setback.

6. Explore Additional Sources of Income:

- Explore opportunities to increase your income temporarily to supplement your existing earnings.

- Take on extra work, freelance projects, part-time jobs, or gig economy jobs to generate additional income during the financial setback.

7. Use Available Resources and Support:

- Utilize available resources such as savings, emergency funds, or other financial assets to cover expenses or bridge income gaps.
- Seek support from family members, friends, or community organizations for assistance or guidance during difficult times.

8. Avoid Borrowing Unnecessarily:

- Be cautious about borrowing money or taking on additional debt to address the financial setback, especially if you're already struggling with debt.
- Consider the long-term implications of borrowing on your financial situation and prioritize sustainable solutions.

9. Seek Professional Help if Needed:

- Consider seeking guidance from a financial advisor, counselor, or planner who can provide personalized advice and strategies for managing financial setbacks.
- A professional can help you develop a tailored plan to navigate the

challenges effectively and regain financial stability over time.

10. Learn from the Experience and Plan for the Future:

- Use financial setbacks as learning opportunities to improve your financial preparedness and resilience.
- Review your budget, emergency fund, and financial plan to identify areas for improvement and make adjustments to better handle future setbacks or emergencies.

By taking proactive steps and staying resilient in the face of financial setbacks and emergencies, you can minimize their impact on your financial well-being and position yourself for long-term success. Remember to stay flexible, adaptable, and proactive in managing challenges, and seek support when needed to overcome obstacles effectively.

Staying motivated and committed to budgeting goals

Staying motivated and committed to budgeting goals can be challenging, but with the right strategies and mindset, you can maintain your focus and achieve financial success.

Here are some tips to help you stay motivated and committed to your budgeting goals:

1. Define Your "Why":

- Clarify your reasons for budgeting and financial goals. Understanding your motivations will help you stay focused during challenging times.
- Reflect on the benefits of budgeting, such as reducing debt, achieving financial freedom, saving for a specific goal, or reducing financial stress.

2. Set Clear and Achievable Goals:

- Establish clear and measurable goals that align with your values and priorities.
- Break down larger goals into smaller, manageable milestones to track your progress and celebrate achievements along the way.

3. Create a Vision Board or Visual Reminders:

- Visualize your financial goals by creating a vision board or using visual reminders such as pictures, quotes, or graphs to keep you inspired and motivated.
- Place these reminders in prominent locations where you'll see them regularly, such as on your desk, refrigerator, or bathroom mirror.

4. Track Your Progress Regularly:

- Monitor your progress towards your budgeting goals regularly to

stay motivated and accountable.
- Use budgeting tools, apps, or spreadsheets to track your income, expenses, savings, and debt repayment.
- Review your progress weekly or monthly and adjust your budget or goals as needed to stay on track.

5. Celebrate Small Wins:

- Celebrate each milestone and achievement, no matter how small, to maintain momentum and motivation.
- Reward yourself for reaching goals or sticking to your budget with non-financial rewards such as a relaxing day off, a favorite activity, or a small treat.

6. Find Support and Accountability:

- Surround yourself with supportive friends, family members, or peers who share your financial goals or can provide encouragement and accountability.
- Join online communities, forums, or social media groups focused on budgeting, saving money, or personal finance to connect with like-minded individuals and share experiences.

7. Stay Inspired and Educated:

- Read books, articles, or blogs on personal finance and budgeting to stay inspired and learn new strategies for managing your finances.
- Listen to podcasts, watch videos, or attend workshops and webinars on budgeting, investing, and financial planning to expand your knowledge and stay motivated.

8. Practice Self-Care and Stress Management:

- Take care of your physical and mental well-being by prioritizing self-care activities such as exercise, meditation, hobbies, and spending time with loved ones.
- Manage stress effectively through relaxation techniques, time management, and seeking support from professionals if needed.

9. Stay Flexible and Adapt:

- Be flexible and adaptable in your approach to budgeting and financial goals.
- Accept that setbacks and challenges may occur along the way and view them as opportunities to learn and grow rather than reasons to give up.

10. Visualize Your Future Financial Freedom:

- Imagine the lifestyle you aspire to achieve through effective bud-

geting and financial discipline.
- Visualize the sense of security, freedom, and fulfillment that comes with achieving your financial goals to stay motivated and committed to your budgeting journey.

By implementing these strategies and staying committed to your budgeting goals, you can overcome challenges, maintain your motivation, and achieve financial success over time.

Remember to stay patient, persistent, and proactive in pursuing your financial dreams, and celebrate every step forward along the way.

7

Monitoring and Adjusting Your Budget

Regularly reviewing your budget

Regularly reviewing your budget is essential for staying on track with your financial goals and making adjustments as needed. Here are some reasons why it's important to review your budget regularly:

1. Monitor Spending Habits:

- Regular budget reviews allow you to monitor your spending habits and identify areas where you may be overspending or underspending.
- By tracking your expenses consistently, you can become more aware of your financial behaviors and make informed decisions to align your spending with your priorities.

2. Ensure Accuracy and Accountability:

- Reviewing your budget regularly ensures that your income, expenses, and savings goals are accurately reflected.
- It holds you accountable for your financial decisions and helps you stay disciplined in following your budgeting plan.

3. Identify Opportunities for Improvement:

- Regular budget reviews help you identify opportunities for improvement and optimization in your budget.
- You can identify areas where you can cut back on expenses, negotiate better deals, or reallocate funds to align with your changing financial priorities.

4. Track Progress Toward Goals:

- Reviewing your budget allows you to track your progress toward your financial goals and milestones.
- You can see how close you are to achieving your goals and make adjustments to your budget or savings plan as needed to stay on target.

5. Adapt to Changing Circumstances:

- Life circumstances and financial priorities can change over time. Regular budget reviews enable you to adapt to these changes and make adjustments to your budget accordingly.
- Whether it's a change in income, expenses, or financial goals, reviewing your budget allows you to stay flexible and responsive to evolving circumstances.

6. Prevent Overspending and Debt:

- Regularly reviewing your budget helps you avoid overspending and accumulating debt.
- By staying mindful of your financial limits and monitoring your spending, you can proactively address potential financial pitfalls before they become significant problems.

7. Build Financial Awareness and Discipline:

- Consistent budget reviews foster financial awareness and discipline by keeping you engaged with your financial plan.
- It encourages responsible financial behavior and reinforces positive habits such as saving, budgeting, and prioritizing needs over wants.

8. Improve Communication and Collaboration:

- If you share financial responsibilities with a partner or family members, regular budget reviews facilitate communication and collaboration.

- It allows everyone involved to stay informed about the household finances, contribute ideas, and work together towards common financial goals.

9. Reduce Stress and Anxiety:

- Regular budget reviews can help reduce stress and anxiety associated with financial uncertainty.
- By staying proactive and informed about your financial situation, you can feel more confident and in control of your finances, even during challenging times.

To ensure the effectiveness of your budget reviews, schedule regular check-ins at least once a month or whenever significant changes occur in your financial situation.

Use budgeting tools, apps, or spreadsheets to streamline the process and make it easier to track your progress over time.

Remember that consistency is key, and the more actively you engage with your budget, the more empowered you'll be to achieve your financial goals.

Tracking progress towards financial goals

Tracking progress towards financial goals is crucial for staying motivated and ensuring that you're on the right path to achieving your objectives. Here's how to effectively track your progress towards financial goals:

1. Define Clear and Specific Goals:

- Start by setting clear and specific financial goals that are measurable, achievable, relevant, and time-bound (SMART goals).
- Whether your goals are related to saving for retirement, paying off debt, buying a home, or building an emergency fund, clearly define the desired outcome and timeline.

2. Break Down Goals into Milestones:

- Break down larger financial goals into smaller, manageable milestones or checkpoints.
- Establish specific targets or benchmarks to track your progress over time and celebrate achievements along the way.

3. Use Quantifiable Metrics:

- Choose quantifiable metrics to measure progress towards each financial goal.
- For example, if your goal is to pay off debt, track the total amount of debt owed, the monthly payments made, and the remaining balance.

4. Set Up a Tracking System:

- Implement a tracking system to monitor your progress towards each financial goal.
- Utilize budgeting tools, spreadsheets, or financial apps to record and update relevant data regularly.

5. Establish Regular Review Periods:

- Schedule regular review periods to assess your progress towards financial goals.
- Depending on the timeline of your goals, you may choose to review your progress monthly, quarterly, or annually.

6. Monitor Key Performance Indicators (KPIs):

- Identify key performance indicators (KPIs) that indicate progress towards each financial goal.
- Examples of KPIs may include savings rate, debt-to-income ratio, net worth, investment growth, or percentage of goal achievement.

7. Track Income, Expenses, and Savings:

- Monitor your income, expenses, and savings regularly to ensure they align with your financial goals.

- Track your cash flow to identify areas where you can cut expenses or increase savings to accelerate progress towards your goals.

8. Adjust Strategies as Needed:

- Be flexible and willing to adjust your strategies as needed based on your progress and changing circumstances.
- If you're falling behind on a particular goal, reassess your approach and make necessary adjustments to get back on track.

9. Celebrate Milestones and Achievements:

- Celebrate each milestone and achievement along the way to maintain motivation and momentum.
- Recognize your progress and reward yourself for reaching milestones, no matter how small.

10. Stay Focused on the Long-Term Vision:

- Keep your long-term vision in mind and stay focused on the bigger picture, even during setbacks or challenges.
- Remember why you set your financial goals in the first place and visualize the future outcomes to stay motivated and committed.

11. Seek Support and Accountability:

- Share your financial goals with trusted friends, family members, or a financial advisor for support and accountability.
- Regular check-ins with an accountability partner can help keep you accountable and motivated to stay on track towards achieving your goals.

12. Review and Adjust Regularly:

- Regularly review your progress towards financial goals and adjust your strategies or timelines as needed.
- Be proactive in addressing obstacles or setbacks and seek assistance or guidance if you encounter challenges along the way.

By implementing these strategies and staying committed to tracking your progress towards financial goals, you can increase your likelihood of success and achieve greater financial security and well-being over time.

Remember that consistency, discipline, and perseverance are key to achieving your financial aspirations.

Making necessary adjustments to your budget plan

Making necessary adjustments to your budget plan is essential for ensuring that it remains relevant and effective in helping you achieve your financial goals. Here's how to make adjustments to your budget plan:

1. Regularly Review Your Budget:

- Schedule regular review sessions to assess your budget's performance and identify areas for improvement.
- Aim to review your budget at least once a month or whenever significant changes occur in your financial situation.

2. Track Your Spending:

- Monitor your actual spending compared to your budgeted amounts to identify any discrepancies or overspending.
- Use budgeting tools, apps, or spreadsheets to categorize and track your expenses accurately.

3. Identify Areas for Adjustment:

- Review each budget category and identify areas where adjustments may be necessary.
- Look for patterns of overspending, unexpected expenses, or changes in income that may require modifications to your budget plan.

4. Prioritize Your Financial Goals:

- Reassess your financial goals and priorities to ensure they align with your current needs and circumstances.
- Determine which goals are most important and allocate resources accordingly within your budget.

5. Cut Back on Discretionary Spending:

- Identify discretionary expenses that can be reduced or eliminated to free up funds for more essential needs or savings goals.
- Look for non-essential items or services that you can temporarily forgo or find lower-cost alternatives.

6. Adjust Variable Expenses:

- Review variable expenses such as groceries, dining out, entertainment, and personal care to see where you can make adjustments.
- Consider setting stricter limits or implementing spending caps in certain categories to control discretionary spending.

7. Negotiate Bills and Expenses:

- Explore opportunities to negotiate lower rates or better terms for recurring bills and expenses.

- Contact service providers, creditors, or lenders to inquire about discounts, promotions, or hardship programs that may be available.

8. Increase Income Sources:

- Look for opportunities to increase your income through additional employment, freelance work, side gigs, or passive income streams.
- Explore ways to monetize your skills, hobbies, or assets to generate extra cash to supplement your budget.

9. Reallocate Funds:

- Consider reallocating funds from lower-priority areas of your budget to higher-priority goals or expenses.
- Be strategic in reallocating resources to ensure that you're maximizing the impact on your financial well-being.

10. Prepare for Unexpected Expenses:

- Review your emergency fund and insurance coverage to ensure you're adequately prepared for unexpected expenses or emergencies.
- Adjust your budget to account for irregular or infrequent expenses that may arise throughout the year.

11. Stay Flexible and Adaptive:

- Stay flexible and open-minded when making adjustments to your budget plan.
- Be willing to adapt to changing circumstances, priorities, or financial goals as needed to stay on track towards achieving your objectives.

12. Monitor and Evaluate:

- After making adjustments to your budget, continue to monitor your spending and financial progress.
- Evaluate the effectiveness of your adjustments and make further tweaks or refinements as necessary to optimize your budget plan over time.

By regularly reviewing your budget and making necessary adjustments, you can ensure that your budget remains relevant and aligned with your financial goals and priorities.

Stay proactive, flexible, and committed to managing your finances effectively, and don't hesitate to seek assistance or guidance if you encounter challenges along the way.

Celebrating achievements and milestones

Celebrating achievements and milestones along your financial journey is essential for staying motivated, recognizing your progress, and reinforcing positive behaviors. Here are some ideas for celebrating your financial successes:

1. Set Milestones and Goals:

Establish specific milestones and goals within your financial plan, such as paying off a certain amount of debt, reaching a savings target, or achieving a higher income level.

2. Acknowledge Progress:

- Regularly acknowledge and celebrate incremental progress towards your financial goals.
- Recognize even small achievements, as they contribute to your overall success.

3. Reward Yourself:

- Treat yourself to a reward or indulgence when you reach a significant milestone or goal.
- Choose rewards that align with your values and priorities, such as a special meal, a spa day, or a weekend getaway.

4. Plan Special Activities:

- Plan special activities or experiences to celebrate major financial achievements.
- Consider hosting a celebratory dinner with family or friends, taking a trip to commemorate a milestone, or participating in a meaningful activity that brings you joy.

5. Share Your Success:

- Share your financial achievements with loved ones, friends, or members of your support network.
- Celebrate your successes together and bask in the encouragement and positive energy of those around you.

6. Create a Vision Board:

- Create a vision board or visual representation of your financial goals and achievements.
- Display it in a prominent place where you'll see it regularly as a reminder of your progress and the rewards awaiting you.

7. Document Your Journey:

- Keep a journal or record of your financial journey, including milestones, challenges, and triumphs.
- Reflect on how far you've come and use your experiences to inspire

and motivate yourself in the future.

8. Practice Gratitude:

- Cultivate gratitude for the progress you've made and the opportunities that have helped you along the way.
- Take time to appreciate the resources, support, and lessons that have contributed to your financial success.

9. Share Your Story:

- Share your financial success story with others through social media, blogs, or community forums.
- Inspire and motivate others by sharing your journey, insights, and strategies for achieving financial goals.

10. Give Back:

- Pay it forward by giving back to others or contributing to causes that are meaningful to you.
- Use your financial success as an opportunity to make a positive impact in your community or the world.

11. Reflect and Set New Goals:

- Take time to reflect on your achievements and the lessons learned along the way.
- Use this reflection to inform your future financial goals and aspirations, setting new challenges to continue growing and evolving.

12. Celebrate Non-Financial Achievements:

Remember that financial success is just one aspect of your life. Celebrate non-financial achievements, such as personal growth, relationships, and health, as well.

Celebrating achievements and milestones in your financial journey not only provides motivation and encouragement but also reinforces positive habits and attitudes towards money management.

Embrace each success as a stepping stone towards your larger financial goals and enjoy the journey along the way.

8

Advanced Budgeting Techniques

Exploring advanced budgeting methods (zero-based budgeting, envelope system, etc.)

Exploring advanced budgeting methods can help you take control of your finances, optimize your spending, and achieve your financial goals more effectively. Here are some advanced budgeting methods to consider:

1. Zero-Based Budgeting:

- Zero-based budgeting requires you to allocate every dollar of your income towards a specific purpose, ensuring that your income minus expenses equals zero.
- Start by listing all your sources of income and then allocate funds to various expense categories, savings goals, debt payments, and investments until you've accounted for every dollar.
- Adjust your budget as needed each month based on changes in

income, expenses, or financial goals.

2. Envelope System:

- The envelope system involves using cash envelopes to allocate funds for different expense categories, such as groceries, dining out, entertainment, and transportation.
- At the beginning of each month, allocate a specific amount of cash to each envelope based on your budgeted amounts for each category.
- Only use cash from the designated envelopes for their respective expenses, and once the cash is gone, refrain from spending more in that category until the next month.

3. 50/30/20 Budget:

- The 50/30/20 budgeting method allocates 50% of your income to needs, 30% to wants, and 20% to savings and debt repayment.
- Needs include essential expenses such as housing, utilities, groceries, and transportation.
- Wants encompass discretionary spending on non-essential items like dining out, entertainment, and vacations.
- Savings and debt repayment focus on building an emergency fund, saving for retirement, paying off debt, and investing for the future.

4. Pay Yourself First:

- With the pay yourself first method, you prioritize saving and investing by allocating a portion of your income to savings goals before paying for any other expenses.
- Set up automatic transfers or deductions from your paycheck to a designated savings or investment account.
- Treat your savings contributions as non-negotiable expenses, ensuring that you're consistently building wealth and working towards your financial goals.

5. Value-Based Budgeting:

- Value-based budgeting involves aligning your spending with your values and priorities to maximize fulfillment and happiness.
- Identify your core values and what matters most to you in life, such as family, health, personal growth, or experiences.
- Allocate your resources towards expenses and activities that align with your values, while minimizing spending on things that don't bring you joy or fulfillment.

6. Bi-Weekly Budgeting:

- Bi-weekly budgeting involves aligning your budget with your bi-weekly pay schedule, allowing you to manage expenses and cash flow more effectively.
- Break down your monthly expenses into two pay periods, adjusting for bills that are due at the beginning or end of the month.
- Allocate funds from each paycheck towards specific expense

categories, savings goals, and debt payments to ensure that you're covering all your financial obligations throughout the month.

7. Priority-Based Budgeting:

- Priority-based budgeting focuses on allocating resources towards your highest-priority expenses and goals first, ensuring that essential needs are met before discretionary spending.
- Identify your top financial priorities, such as debt repayment, emergency savings, retirement contributions, or specific savings goals.
- Allocate a significant portion of your income towards these priorities, adjusting discretionary spending as needed to accommodate your highest-priority goals.

8. The 60% Solution:

- The 60% solution budgeting method involves allocating 60% of your income towards fixed expenses, 10% towards savings, and 30% towards flexible spending.
- Fixed expenses include housing, utilities, transportation, insurance premiums, and debt payments.
- Savings encompass contributions to emergency savings, retirement accounts, and other long-term financial goals.
- Flexible spending covers discretionary expenses such as groceries, dining out, entertainment, and personal care.

9. Budgeting with Multiple Accounts:

- Use multiple bank accounts to segregate funds for different purposes, such as bills, savings goals, discretionary spending, and irregular expenses.
- Set up automated transfers to move money into each account based on your budgeted amounts for each category.
- Track your spending and account balances to ensure that you're staying within budget and effectively managing your cash flow.

10. Advanced Tracking and Analytics:

- Utilize advanced budgeting tools, apps, or software that offer robust tracking and analytics features.
- Look for tools that allow you to categorize transactions, track spending trends over time, set custom alerts and reminders, and generate detailed reports.
- Analyze your financial data to identify patterns, opportunities for improvement, and areas where you can optimize your budgeting strategies.

11. Continuous Improvement:

- Continuously evaluate and refine your budgeting methods to improve effectiveness and efficiency.
- Experiment with different approaches, techniques, and tools to

find what works best for your unique financial situation and goals.
- Be open to learning from your experiences and making adjustments as needed to achieve greater financial success and stability over time.

By exploring advanced budgeting methods and incorporating them into your financial planning, you can gain greater control over your finances, optimize your spending, and make meaningful progress towards your financial goals.

Choose the methods that resonate most with your preferences, lifestyle, and objectives, and be proactive in implementing them consistently to achieve long-term financial success.

Strategies for long-term financial planning (retirement savings, investments, etc.)

Long-term financial planning is essential for achieving financial security and independence over the years. Here are some strategies for long-term financial planning, including retirement savings, investments, and more:

1. Start Early:

- Begin saving and investing for long-term goals as early as possible to take advantage of the power of compounding.
- Even small contributions made early on can grow significantly over time, thanks to the effects of compounding returns.

2. Set Clear Goals:

- Define your long-term financial goals, such as retirement, home-ownership, education funding, or wealth accumulation.
- Quantify your goals by determining the amount of money you'll need and the timeframe in which you aim to achieve them.

3. Establish an Emergency Fund:

- Build an emergency fund to cover unexpected expenses or financial setbacks.
- Aim to save 3-6 months' worth of living expenses in a liquid, easily accessible account for emergencies.

4. Contribute to Retirement Accounts:

- Maximize contributions to tax-advantaged retirement accounts such as 401(k)s, IRAs, or Roth IRAs.
- Take advantage of employer-sponsored retirement plans and matching contributions to boost your retirement savings.

5. Diversify Investments:

- Diversify your investment portfolio across different asset classes,

such as stocks, bonds, real estate, and alternative investments.
- Asset allocation should be based on your risk tolerance, time horizon, and financial goals.

6. Utilize Tax-Efficient Strategies:

- Consider tax-efficient investment strategies to minimize taxes and maximize after-tax returns.
- Invest in tax-advantaged accounts, tax-deferred investments, and tax-efficient funds to optimize your tax situation.

7. Automate Savings and Investments:

- Set up automatic contributions to retirement accounts and investment accounts to ensure consistent saving and investing.
- Automating contributions makes it easier to stay disciplined and maintain a regular saving and investing habit.

8. Rebalance Your Portfolio Regularly:

- Rebalance your investment portfolio periodically to maintain your desired asset allocation and risk level.
- Adjust your portfolio as needed based on changes in market conditions, your financial situation, or your investment objectives.

9. Stay Informed and Educated:

- Stay informed about financial markets, economic trends, and investment opportunities through ongoing education and research.
- Continuously seek to improve your financial literacy and investment knowledge to make informed decisions.

10. Seek Professional Advice:

- Consider working with a financial advisor or planner to develop a comprehensive long-term financial plan tailored to your goals and circumstances.
- A professional advisor can provide personalized guidance, portfolio management, and strategic advice to help you achieve your financial objectives.

11. Monitor and Review Progress:

- Regularly monitor your progress towards long-term financial goals and adjust your plan as needed.
- Review your investments, savings rates, and overall financial strategy on an annual basis or whenever significant life changes occur.

12. Plan for Estate and Legacy:

- Develop an estate plan to ensure your assets are distributed according to your wishes and minimize taxes upon your passing.
- Consider legacy planning to leave a lasting impact through charitable giving, philanthropy, or other forms of wealth transfer.

13. Maintain Adequate Insurance Coverage:

- Protect your financial future by maintaining adequate insurance coverage, including life insurance, health insurance, disability insurance, and long-term care insurance.
- Review your insurance needs regularly and adjust coverage as necessary to reflect changes in your life circumstances.

14. Stay Disciplined and Patient:

- Long-term financial planning requires discipline, patience, and a long-term perspective.
- Stay committed to your financial goals, resist the urge to react impulsively to short-term market fluctuations, and remain focused on the bigger picture.

By implementing these strategies for long-term financial planning, you can build a solid foundation for financial security, achieve your goals, and enjoy peace of mind knowing that you're prepared for the future.

Remember that long-term success requires diligence, patience, and adaptability, so stay committed to your plan and be proactive in managing your finances effectively over time.

Incorporating budgeting into lifestyle changes (marriage, parenthood, career changes, etc.)

Incorporating budgeting into lifestyle changes such as marriage, parenthood, career changes, or other significant life events is crucial for maintaining financial stability and achieving your financial goals. Here are some strategies for integrating budgeting into these lifestyle transitions:

1. Marriage:

- Communicate openly and honestly with your partner about your financial values, goals, and priorities.
- Merge your finances or establish a system for managing joint expenses, savings, and investments.
- Create a shared budget that reflects your combined income, expenses, and financial goals.
- Set aside time regularly to review your budget together and make adjustments as needed to accommodate changes in your lifestyle or financial circumstances.
- Establish clear guidelines for spending, saving, and decision-making to ensure transparency and accountability in your financial partnership.

2. Parenthood:

- Anticipate and plan for the financial impact of parenthood, including expenses related to childcare, education, healthcare, and other child-rearing costs.
- Adjust your budget to accommodate new expenses and prioritize saving for your child's future needs, such as education funds or a college savings plan.
- Look for ways to reduce discretionary spending and reallocate funds towards childcare expenses or other parenting priorities.
- Consider childcare options, such as daycare, nanny services, or flexible work arrangements, that align with your budget and lifestyle.
- Review your insurance coverage and estate plan to ensure that your family's financial future is protected in the event of unforeseen circumstances.

3. Career Changes:

- Evaluate the financial implications of career changes, such as job transitions, promotions, salary changes, or starting a new business.
- Adjust your budget to reflect changes in income, benefits, and expenses associated with your new career path.
- Build a financial cushion or emergency fund to cover any potential income disruptions during periods of career transition or uncertainty.
- Consider the long-term impact of career decisions on your financial goals, retirement plans, and overall financial well-being.
- Seek professional guidance or advice from a financial advisor to help you navigate the financial aspects of career changes and make informed decisions.

4. Major Life Events:

- Prepare for major life events such as buying a home, relocating, starting a family, or caring for aging parents by incorporating them into your budgeting process.
- Anticipate one-time expenses associated with these life events and save accordingly to avoid financial strain.
- Review your budget regularly to assess how major life events may impact your financial goals and adjust your plan accordingly.
- Seek out resources, support, and guidance from financial professionals or community organizations to help you navigate the financial aspects of major life changes.
- Stay flexible and adaptable in your budgeting approach, recognizing that life events may require adjustments to your financial plan over time.

5. Maintain Open Communication:

- Maintain open communication with your partner, family members, or support network about your financial goals, challenges, and priorities.
- Discuss any changes or adjustments to your budgeting plan openly and collaboratively to ensure that everyone is on the same page.
- Seek input, feedback, and support from loved ones as you navigate budgeting and lifestyle changes together.

6. Be Flexible and Adaptable:

- Be prepared to adjust your budgeting strategies and priorities as needed to accommodate changes in your lifestyle, goals, or financial circumstances.
- Embrace flexibility and adaptability in your budgeting approach, recognizing that life is dynamic and ever-changing.
- Stay proactive and proactive in managing your finances, and be willing to seek out resources or assistance when needed to overcome challenges or obstacles.

Incorporating budgeting into lifestyle changes requires proactive planning, open communication, and flexibility to adapt to new circumstances.

By integrating budgeting into major life events and transitions, you can maintain financial stability, achieve your goals, and navigate life's changes with confidence and peace of mind.

Tips for maintaining financial discipline and avoiding budgeting pitfalls

Maintaining financial discipline and avoiding budgeting pitfalls requires commitment, self-awareness, and proactive planning. Here are some tips to help you stay on track with your budget and avoid common pitfalls:

1. Set Clear Financial Goals:

- Define your financial goals and priorities, whether it's paying off debt, saving for a down payment, or building an emergency fund.

- Having clear goals provides motivation and direction for your budgeting efforts.

2. Create a Realistic Budget:

- Develop a budget that reflects your income, expenses, and financial goals.
- Be realistic about your spending habits and set achievable targets for each expense category.

3. Track Your Spending:

- Monitor your spending regularly to ensure that you're staying within your budget.
- Use budgeting apps, spreadsheets, or pen-and-paper methods to track your expenses and identify areas for improvement.

4. Practice Delayed Gratification:

- Avoid impulse purchases and practice delayed gratification by waiting before making non-essential purchases.
- Give yourself time to consider whether a purchase aligns with your financial goals and budget before committing to it.

5. Separate Needs from Wants:

- Distinguish between essential needs and discretionary wants when budgeting.
- Prioritize spending on needs such as housing, food, and transportation before allocating funds to wants like dining out or entertainment.

6. Build an Emergency Fund:

- Set aside funds in an emergency savings account to cover unexpected expenses or financial emergencies.
- Aim to save 3-6 months' worth of living expenses to provide a financial buffer in case of job loss, medical bills, or other unforeseen circumstances.

7. Avoid Lifestyle Inflation:

- Resist the temptation to increase your spending as your income grows.
- Instead, allocate extra income towards savings, investments, or debt repayment to accelerate your progress towards financial goals.

8. Use Cash or Debit Cards:

- Limit your use of credit cards to prevent overspending and accumulating debt.
- Consider using cash or debit cards for everyday purchases to help you stay within your budget and avoid interest charges.

9. Review Your Budget Regularly:

- Schedule regular budget reviews to assess your progress, identify areas for improvement, and make necessary adjustments.
- Update your budget as needed to reflect changes in your income, expenses, or financial goals.

10. Plan for Irregular Expenses:

- Anticipate irregular expenses such as annual subscriptions, car maintenance, or holiday gifts, and budget for them accordingly.
- Set aside funds each month in a separate savings account or budget category to cover these expenses when they arise.

11. Seek Support and Accountability:

- Share your financial goals and challenges with a trusted friend, family member, or financial advisor for support and accountability.
- Consider joining a budgeting group or community for additional encouragement and motivation.

12. Learn from Mistakes:

- Accept that mistakes may happen along your financial journey and view them as opportunities for learning and growth.
- Identify the factors that led to budgeting pitfalls or overspending and adjust your approach accordingly to prevent similar issues in the future.

13. Celebrate Progress:

- Celebrate achievements and milestones along your financial journey to stay motivated and reinforce positive behaviors.
- Acknowledge your progress, no matter how small, and celebrate your accomplishments as you work towards your financial goals.

14. Stay Focused on Long-Term Success:

- Keep your long-term financial goals in mind and stay committed to achieving them, even when faced with short-term challenges or temptations.
- Remind yourself of the benefits of financial discipline, such as increased financial security, reduced stress, and greater freedom to pursue your passions and dreams.

By following these tips and staying disciplined with your budgeting efforts, you can maintain financial discipline, avoid common pitfalls, and achieve greater success in managing your finances effectively over time.

Remember that consistency, perseverance, and self-awareness are key to long-term financial well-being.

9

Building Wealth and Achieving Financial Freedom

S**trategies for building wealth over time**

Building wealth over time requires a combination of disciplined saving, strategic investing, and smart financial decision-making. Here are some strategies to help you build wealth gradually and sustainably:

1. Set Clear Financial Goals:

- Define your long-term financial goals, whether it's achieving financial independence, retiring early, buying a home, or starting a business.
- Break down your goals into smaller, actionable steps and timelines to make them more achievable.

2. Develop a Comprehensive Financial Plan:

- Create a detailed financial plan that outlines your income, expenses, savings goals, investment strategy, and debt management plan.
- Consider working with a financial advisor to develop a personalized plan tailored to your goals, risk tolerance, and financial situation.

3. Save Consistently:

- Make saving a priority by consistently setting aside a portion of your income for savings and investments.
- Automate your savings contributions to ensure they're deposited into designated accounts regularly, such as retirement accounts, brokerage accounts, or high-yield savings accounts.

4. Live Below Your Means:

- Practice frugality and live below your means by spending less than you earn.
- Avoid lifestyle inflation and unnecessary expenses, and prioritize saving and investing the difference to grow your wealth over time.

5. Invest Wisely:

- Develop a diversified investment strategy that aligns with your financial goals, risk tolerance, and time horizon.
- Invest in a mix of asset classes, such as stocks, bonds, real estate, and alternative investments, to spread risk and maximize returns.
- Take advantage of tax-advantaged accounts such as 401(k)s, IRAs, and Health Savings Accounts (HSAs) to minimize taxes and maximize growth potential.

6. Maximize Retirement Contributions:

- Contribute the maximum amount allowed to your employer-sponsored retirement plan, such as a 401(k) or 403(b), especially if your employer offers matching contributions.
- Take advantage of catch-up contributions if you're over the age of 50 to accelerate your retirement savings.

7. Pay Off High-Interest Debt:

- Prioritize paying off high-interest debt, such as credit card debt or personal loans, to reduce interest costs and free up funds for saving and investing.
- Consider debt consolidation or refinancing options to lower interest rates and streamline debt repayment.

8. Build Multiple Income Streams:

- Diversify your income sources by building multiple streams of income, such as rental income, passive investment income, freelance work, or side businesses.
- Explore opportunities to monetize your skills, hobbies, or expertise to generate additional income outside of your primary job.

9. Continuously Educate Yourself:

- Stay informed about personal finance, investing, and wealth-building strategies by reading books, attending seminars, and following reputable financial publications.
- Continuously educate yourself about investment options, market trends, and economic developments to make informed decisions about your finances.

10. Take Calculated Risks:

- Be willing to take calculated risks with your investments to achieve higher returns over the long term.
- Conduct thorough research, diversify your portfolio, and avoid speculative or high-risk investments that could jeopardize your financial security.

11. Plan for Taxes and Inflation:

- Factor in taxes and inflation when planning your finances and investment strategy.
- Consider tax-efficient investment strategies and investment vehicles that offer protection against inflation to preserve your purchasing power over time.

12. Stay Disciplined and Patient:

- Building wealth is a marathon, not a sprint. Stay disciplined, patient, and focused on your long-term goals, even during periods of market volatility or economic uncertainty.
- Avoid making impulsive decisions based on short-term market fluctuations, and maintain a long-term perspective on investing and wealth-building.

13. Review and Adjust Regularly:

- Regularly review your financial plan, investment portfolio, and progress towards your goals.
- Adjust your strategy as needed based on changes in your financial situation, goals, or market conditions to stay on track towards building wealth over time.

By implementing these strategies and staying committed to your financial goals, you can build wealth gradually and achieve greater financial security and independence over the long term. Remember that building wealth requires patience, discipline, and consistent effort, but the rewards can be substantial and life-changing in the future.

Setting and achieving financial milestones

Setting and achieving financial milestones is key to building wealth over time and achieving long-term financial success. Here are some strategies to help you set and reach your financial milestones:

1. Define Clear and Specific Goals:

Start by defining your financial goals in clear and specific terms. Whether it's buying a home, paying off debt, saving for retirement, or starting a business, articulate your objectives with clarity.

2. Break Down Goals into Smaller Milestones:

Break down larger financial goals into smaller, manageable milestones or checkpoints. This allows you to track your progress more effectively and maintain momentum along the way.

3. Set SMART Goals:

Ensure that your financial goals are SMART: Specific, Measurable, Achievable, Relevant, and Time-bound. This framework helps you create goals that are realistic and actionable.

4. Prioritize Your Goals:

Prioritize your financial goals based on their importance and urgency. Identify which goals are short-term, medium-term, and long-term, and allocate your resources accordingly.

5. Create a Plan:

Develop a strategic plan for achieving each financial milestone. Break down the steps you need to take, estimate the time and resources required, and establish deadlines for completion.

6. Track Your Progress:

Regularly track your progress towards each financial milestone. Monitor your income, expenses, savings, investments, and debt repayment to ensure that you're on track to meet your goals.

7. Celebrate Achievements:

Celebrate each milestone and achievement along the way. Recognize your progress and reward yourself for reaching important financial goals, no matter how small.

8. Stay Flexible:

Be flexible and adaptable in your approach to achieving financial milestones. Life circumstances and priorities may change, so be prepared to adjust your goals and strategies accordingly.

9. Stay Motivated:

Stay motivated and focused on your financial goals by reminding yourself of the benefits of achieving them. Visualize your success, stay positive, and surround yourself with supportive people who encourage your progress.

10. Seek Support and Accountability:

Share your financial goals with trusted friends, family members, or a financial advisor for support and accountability. Having someone to hold you accountable can help you stay committed to your goals.

11. Review and Adjust:

Regularly review your financial goals and progress, and make adjustments as needed. If you encounter obstacles or setbacks, reassess your plan and make necessary changes to keep moving forward.

12. Maintain Discipline:

Stay disciplined in your financial habits and decisions. Avoid unnecessary spending, stick to your budget, and prioritize your financial goals over short-term gratification.

13. Stay Informed:

Stay informed about personal finance topics, investment strategies, and financial planning best practices. Continuous learning can help you make informed decisions and optimize your financial strategies over time.

14. Plan for the Unexpected:

Prepare for unexpected events or emergencies that may impact your financial journey. Maintain an emergency fund, adequate insurance coverage, and a contingency plan to mitigate risks.

By implementing these strategies and staying committed to your financial goals, you can set and achieve meaningful financial milestones that lead to long-term wealth and financial security.

Remember that building wealth takes time, patience, and consistent effort, but with careful planning and perseverance, you can achieve financial success over time.

Achieving financial independence and early retirement

Achieving financial independence and early retirement, often referred to as FIRE (Financial Independence, Retire Early), requires careful planning, disciplined saving, and strategic investing. Here are some strategies to help you pursue financial independence and early retirement:

1. Determine Your Financial Independence Number:

Calculate your financial independence number, also known as your "retirement number" or "FIRE number." This is the amount of money you need to cover your expenses without needing to work for income.

2. Save Aggressively:

- Aim to save a high percentage of your income, typically 50% or more, to accelerate your path to financial independence.

- Cut unnecessary expenses, prioritize saving and investing, and live below your means to maximize your savings rate.

3. Invest Wisely:

- Invest your savings in a diversified portfolio of low-cost index funds, stocks, bonds, real estate, or other assets with long-term growth potential.
- Consider tax-advantaged retirement accounts such as 401(k)s, IRAs, and HSAs to maximize tax benefits and accelerate your investment growth.

4. Follow the 4% Rule:

- Utilize the 4% rule as a guideline for determining a sustainable withdrawal rate from your investment portfolio in retirement.
- Withdraw 4% of your portfolio balance annually, adjusted for inflation, to maintain a consistent standard of living without depleting your savings.

5. Create Multiple Income Streams:

- Diversify your income sources to reduce reliance on a single source of income.

- Explore side hustles, freelance work, rental income, dividend-paying stocks, or other passive income streams to supplement your savings and support your financial independence goals.

6. Consider Geographic Arbitrage:

- Take advantage of geographic arbitrage by living in areas with lower costs of living or favorable tax environments.
- Moving to a more affordable location can stretch your savings further and accelerate your path to financial independence.

7. Pay Off Debt:

- Prioritize paying off high-interest debt, such as credit cards or student loans, to reduce financial burdens and free up more cash flow for saving and investing.
- Consider refinancing or consolidating debt to lower interest rates and accelerate debt repayment.

8. Practice Frugal Living:

- Embrace frugal living habits by minimizing unnecessary expenses, shopping mindfully, and finding ways to maximize value without overspending.
- Focus on experiences, relationships, and personal fulfillment rather

than material possessions.

9. Continuously Monitor Your Progress:

- Regularly review your financial goals, track your savings and investment progress, and adjust your plan as needed to stay on track.
- Use financial independence calculators or retirement planning tools to assess your progress towards your FIRE goals.

10. Plan for Healthcare Costs:

- Factor healthcare costs into your early retirement plan and explore options for obtaining affordable health insurance coverage.
- Consider Health Savings Accounts (HSAs) or other healthcare savings vehicles to cover medical expenses in retirement.

11. Be Prepared for Contingencies:

- Build a financial safety net to cover unexpected expenses or emergencies that may arise during early retirement.
- Maintain an emergency fund and consider purchasing disability insurance or long-term care insurance for additional protection.

12. Transition to Early Retirement Gradually:

- Consider a phased or gradual transition to early retirement, allowing you to test the waters, adjust your lifestyle, and mitigate financial risks before fully retiring.
- Explore flexible work arrangements, part-time employment, or consulting opportunities to generate income while enjoying greater freedom and flexibility.

13. Seek Professional Guidance:

- Consult with a financial advisor or planner who specializes in early retirement planning to develop a personalized strategy tailored to your goals and circumstances.
- A professional advisor can provide guidance on tax planning, investment strategies, withdrawal strategies, and other key aspects of early retirement planning.

14. Stay Flexible and Adaptable:

- Stay flexible and adaptable in your early retirement plan, recognizing that circumstances may change over time.
- Be prepared to adjust your goals, strategies, and expectations as needed to navigate unexpected challenges or opportunities along your journey to financial independence.

By following these strategies and staying disciplined in your approach, you can pursue financial independence and early retirement on your own terms.

Remember that early retirement requires careful planning, sacrifice, and commitment, but the rewards of financial freedom and lifestyle flexibility can make it well worth the effort.

Tips for sustaining financial success in the long run

Sustaining financial success in the long run requires a combination of prudent financial management, disciplined habits, and a strategic mindset. Here are some tips to help you maintain and grow your financial success over time:

1. Continuously Monitor and Review Your Finances:

- Regularly review your financial situation, including your income, expenses, savings, investments, and debts.
- Monitor your progress towards your financial goals and make adjustments to your plan as needed.

2. Stick to Your Budget:

- Maintain discipline with your budgeting habits and avoid over-spending.
- Regularly track your expenses and ensure that you're living within your means.

3. Save and Invest Wisely:

- Continue to prioritize saving and investing for the long term.
- Diversify your investment portfolio and focus on strategies that align with your risk tolerance and financial goals.

4. Build Multiple Income Streams:

- Explore opportunities to diversify your income sources, such as starting a side business, freelancing, or investing in rental properties.
- Having multiple streams of income can provide stability and resilience in uncertain economic conditions.

5. Protect Your Assets:

- Maintain adequate insurance coverage to protect your assets and mitigate financial risks.
- Review your insurance policies regularly to ensure that they meet your current needs and circumstances.

6. Plan for Retirement:

- Continue to save for retirement even after achieving financial independence.

- Regularly review your retirement savings strategy and adjust your contributions as needed to stay on track towards your retirement goals.

7. Stay Educated:

- Stay informed about personal finance topics, investment strategies, and economic trends.
- Continuously educate yourself to make informed financial decisions and adapt to changes in the financial landscape.

8. Manage Debt Wisely:

- Avoid accumulating unnecessary debt and focus on paying off high-interest debt as quickly as possible.
- Use debt strategically, such as leveraging low-interest loans for investments that have the potential to generate higher returns.

9. Plan for Taxes:

- Develop tax-efficient strategies to minimize your tax burden and maximize your after-tax returns.
- Take advantage of tax-advantaged retirement accounts, investment vehicles, and deductions to optimize your tax situation.

10. Prepare for the Unexpected:

- Build an emergency fund to cover unexpected expenses or financial setbacks.
- Have a contingency plan in place to deal with unforeseen circumstances such as job loss, illness, or economic downturns.

11. Practice Long-Term Thinking:

- Maintain a long-term perspective with your financial decisions and avoid succumbing to short-term impulses.
- Focus on your overarching financial goals and make decisions that support your long-term financial well-being.

12. Seek Professional Advice:

- Consider working with a financial advisor or planner to develop a comprehensive financial plan tailored to your needs and goals.
- A professional advisor can provide personalized guidance, portfolio management, and strategic advice to help you navigate complex financial situations.

13. Stay Disciplined and Patient:

- Remain disciplined in your financial habits and patient in your investment approach.
- Recognize that building wealth and achieving financial success takes time, consistency, and perseverance.

14. Give Back:

- Consider giving back to your community or supporting charitable causes once you've achieved financial success.
- Giving back can provide a sense of purpose and fulfillment, while also making a positive impact on the lives of others.

By following these tips and maintaining good financial habits, you can sustain financial success in the long run and enjoy a secure and prosperous future.

Remember that financial success is a journey, not a destination, and it requires ongoing effort and commitment to maintain and grow over time.

10

Conclusion

Recap of key budgeting principles and strategies

Here's a recap of key budgeting principles and strategies to help you effectively manage your finances:

Budgeting Principles:

- Track Your Income and Expenses: Keep track of your income sources and all expenses to understand where your money is coming from and where it's going.
- Differentiate Between Needs and Wants: Prioritize essential expenses (needs) over discretionary spending (wants) to ensure you cover your basic necessities first.
- Set Financial Goals: Establish short-term and long-term financial goals to provide direction and motivation for your budgeting efforts.
- Live Within Your Means: Spend less than you earn to avoid

accumulating debt and maintain financial stability.

- Build an Emergency Fund: Set aside funds for unexpected expenses or financial emergencies to avoid dipping into savings or going into debt.
- Plan for Irregular Expenses: Anticipate irregular expenses such as car repairs or annual subscriptions and budget for them accordingly.
- Review and Adjust Regularly: Regularly review your budget, track your progress towards financial goals, and make adjustments as needed to stay on track.

Budgeting Strategies:

- Zero-Based Budgeting: Allocate every dollar of your income to a specific expense or savings category, ensuring that your income minus expenses equals zero.
- Envelope System: Allocate cash into envelopes for different expense categories, such as groceries, entertainment, and transportation, to control discretionary spending.
- 50/30/20 Rule: Allocate 50% of your income to needs, 30% to wants, and 20% to savings and debt repayment to maintain a balanced budget.
- Pay Yourself First: Prioritize savings by automatically setting aside a portion of your income for savings and investments before paying for other expenses.
- Value-Based Budgeting: Align your spending with your values and priorities to maximize fulfillment and happiness while minimizing non-essential expenses.
- Bi-Weekly Budgeting: Align your budget with your bi-weekly pay

schedule, budgeting expenses accordingly for each pay period to manage cash flow effectively.

- Priority-Based Budgeting: Allocate resources towards your highest-priority expenses and goals first, ensuring essential needs are met before discretionary spending.
- The 60% Solution: Allocate 60% of your income to fixed expenses, 10% to savings, and 30% to flexible spending to maintain a balanced budget.

By incorporating these principles and strategies into your budgeting approach, you can gain better control over your finances, achieve your financial goals, and build a solid foundation for long-term financial success.

Remember, budgeting is a dynamic process that requires ongoing attention and adjustment to reflect changes in your financial situation and goals.

Encouragement to take control of finances and pursue financial goals

Taking control of your finances and pursuing your financial goals can be one of the most empowering and rewarding decisions you'll ever make. Here's some encouragement to inspire you on your journey:

1. Empower Yourself:

Remember that you have the power to shape your financial future. By taking control of your finances, you're taking control of your life and paving the way for a brighter tomorrow.

2. Focus on What's Possible:

No matter where you are right now, know that there's always room for improvement. Your financial situation is not fixed; it's dynamic and can change for the better with the right mindset and actions.

3. Believe in Your Ability to Succeed:

Believe in yourself and your ability to achieve your financial goals. Your past does not define your future, and with determination and perseverance, you can overcome any obstacle standing in your way.

4. Take Small Steps:

Rome wasn't built in a day, and neither will your financial success be. Break down your goals into smaller, manageable steps, and focus on taking consistent action every day to move closer to your objectives.

5. Learn and Grow:

Take the time to educate yourself about personal finance, budgeting, investing, and wealth-building strategies. Knowledge is power, and the more you know, the better equipped you'll be to make informed financial decisions.

6. Embrace Challenges:

Challenges are inevitable on the road to financial success, but they're also opportunities for growth and learning. Embrace challenges as a chance to become stronger, wiser, and more resilient.

7. Celebrate Progress:

Celebrate every milestone and achievement along the way, no matter how small. Each step forward is a victory worth celebrating and a reminder of how far you've come.

8. Stay Positive and Persistent:

Stay positive, even when faced with setbacks or obstacles. Remember that setbacks are temporary, and with persistence and determination, you can overcome them and keep moving forward.

9. Surround Yourself with Support:

Surround yourself with supportive people who believe in you and your goals. Seek out mentors, friends, or family members who can offer encouragement, guidance, and accountability.

10. Visualize Your Success:

Visualize yourself achieving your financial goals and living the life you desire. Use visualization techniques to reinforce your belief in your ability to succeed and stay motivated on your journey.

11. Practice Gratitude:

Cultivate gratitude for what you have and the progress you've made so far. Gratitude can shift your focus from what you lack to what you have and create a positive mindset for achieving even more.

12. Take Action Today:

Don't wait for the perfect moment to start; the perfect moment is now. Take action today, even if it's a small step, and commit to making progress towards your financial goals every single day.

Remember, your financial future is in your hands, and the choices you make today will shape the life you live tomorrow.

Believe in yourself, stay focused on your goals, and keep moving forward with confidence and determination.

You have the power to create the financial future you desire—go out there and make it happen!

Final words of motivation and inspiration

As you embark on your journey towards financial freedom and success, remember that every step you take brings you closer to your goals. Stay focused, stay determined, and never underestimate the power of your own resilience and determination.

There will be challenges along the way, but with each challenge comes an opportunity for growth and learning. Embrace these challenges as stepping stones to your success, and never lose sight of the vision you have for your future.

You have everything within you to achieve your dreams. Believe in yourself, trust in your abilities, and keep pushing forward, even when the path seems difficult. Your perseverance and dedication will lead you to extraordinary heights.

Above all, remember to enjoy the journey. Celebrate your victories, no matter how small, and cherish the progress you've made. Your journey towards financial success is not just about reaching the destination—it's about the experiences, the lessons learned, and the person you become along the way.

So keep dreaming, keep striving, and keep believing in yourself. The best is yet to come, and the future is full of endless possibilities. You have the power to create the life you desire, and I have no doubt that you will achieve greatness.

Go forth with courage, go forth with passion, and go forth with unwavering determination. Your financial success awaits, and I'm excited to see all that you will accomplish. You've got this!

11

Resources

ChatGPT. (n.d.-a). https://chat.openai.com/. Retrieved February 15, 2024, from https://chat.openai.com/

Tim. (2023, February 28). *9 Inspiring budgeting quotes (and how you can use them to take action NOW) - Atypical finance*. Atypical Finance. Retrieved February 15, 2024, from https://www.atypicalfinance.com/9-inspiring-budgeting-quotes-and-how-you-can-use-them-to-take-action-now/